I0558933

The Hive

Multi-Generational Wealth Building: A Guide to Creating a Lasting Legacy

James L. Marshall, Jr.

Cover Art

The name of the piece is "Black Phoenix: Our history of wealth" The original artwork was commissioned by James Marshall and installed in the Marshall Building in 2002. The work symbolizes our journey from slavery to business ownership; from being a commodity, to owning buildings. Historical figures depicted in the artwork are: Booker T. Washington, George Carver Washington, Marcus Garvey, Madame C. J. Walker and the founders of Black Wall Street in Tulsa, Ok.

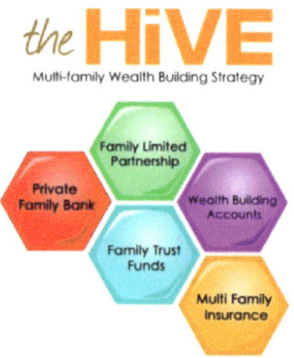

the **HiVE**
Multi-family Wealth Building Strategy

Family Limited Partnership

Private Family Bank

Wealth Building Accounts

Family Trust Funds

Multi Family Insurance

A Journey of a thousand mile starts with one step... **Planning!**

Table of Contents

Foreword by
Winston Pittman, Sr.

This book, *The Hive: Multi-Generational Wealth Building: A Guide to Creating a Lasting Legacy,* by James Marshall, is a significant source of information for everybody who desires to build something lasting for their immediate and extended family. I encourage everyone to read it and not sleep on this treasure! James has been my trusted financial advisor for more than twenty years. With his expert guidance, I have implemented the strategies to transfer my family's wealth to multiple generations. No one makes it alone, and certainly not me.

My great-grandfather came out of slavery, so it all started with him. When he was free, he eventually bought 375 acres of land in Mississippi. He had 18 kids, and one of them, my grandfather, took after his father. My grandfather bought 1,100 acres of land and became an entrepreneur by buying timber. He eventually was one of the wealthiest men in the county. My father picked up where my grandfather left off by becoming a contractor and building churches in Mississippi. Well, I guess it just passed on to me.

I know everything I have is a gift from God and made possible by the financial foundation provided by my forefathers. Everything I've done and the talent I have is a gift, and I have taken those talents and polished them. One of the hardest things I've accomplished in my life was establishing my business, and I love what I do. And even if I fail, I am convinced I will get it all back, and then some, in half the time because of the legacy of excellence my forefathers instilled in me and all the knowledge I have accumulated along the way.

I urge you to read this book from cover to cover, absorbing every word with an open mind and a spirit of acceptance. By doing so, you equip yourself with the necessary knowledge and insights to embark on your family's multi-generational wealth-building journey.

Introduction

"At the bottom of education, at the bottom of politics, even at the bottom of religion, there must be for our race economic independence."

–Booker T. Washington

Generational wealth is the accumulation of assets passed down from generation to generation. Assets are items, property, and other things that hold immediate value and have the opportunity to increase in value. It can include anything from cash and investments to real estate and businesses. While it is possible to build generational wealth in a single lifetime, it is often more sustainable and successful when it is built over multiple generations. In other words, someone plants a tree that they will not live to see fully grown. And that takes vision, discipline and commitment!

Building multi-generational wealth has many benefits. For one, it can provide a sense of security and stability for future generations by giving them a stable financial foundation to build on. This is especially true when families commit to the concept of multi-generational wealth and put their resources behind the effort. Additionally, multi-generational wealth can be used to promote charitable giving and other philanthropic activities. However, this book aims to suggest a solution for bridging the wealth gap without using many unnecessary words, or what I like to call "word salad." I want to pique your interest enough to encourage you to learn more about wealth building and wealth transfer. Hopefully, you will contact a financial professional to guide your wealth-building and transfer journey.

What I have realized after more than 35 years of advising clients about building wealth and investing their assets, as well as educating the community about basic financial management, is that we are not taking this thing seriously enough! When I traced my family tree back to Sarah Moore 1874, James Young 1872, Mary Barnett 1876, and Richard Marshall 1873, I realized how great a loss the opportunity of multi-generational wealth has been in my own family.

According to my calculations, using very modest insurance policies of $40,000 on average over the last 99 years, my family cooperative trust should be valued at approximately $100,000,000 (100 hundred million dollars). Consequently, I wrote this book to encourage everyone who reads it to start acting today. It will forever change the financial dynamics of their immediate and extended family for generations.

We spend a lot of time talking and complaining about the problem of disproportionate wealth distribution and why things are the way they are. We should continue talking about it so that those who don't know or don't fully understand the concepts of generational wealth building can be educated. However, more effort must be poured into action. No matter how long it takes, keep taking positive and constructive steps toward the desired solution. Setbacks and missteps will happen. But as long as we learn from them and keep trying, things will change.

Of course, there are challenges to building multi-generational wealth. One is that it requires a long-term perspective. It takes time to accumulate wealth and ensure it is managed and invested wisely. Another challenge is that generational wealth can be vulnerable to unforeseen events, such as economic downturns or family disputes. Each of these can be effectively managed by putting the proper structure in place.

Despite the challenges, building multi-generational wealth is a worthwhile goal. It can provide a lasting legacy for your family and help ensure future generations have the resources they need to succeed.

Throughout my financial career, I've talked to thousands of people about money management and wealth building and conducted countless workshops, seminars, and webinars on financial planning and legacy planning. I know for a fact that most people want to be wealthy and leave a legacy; however, their desires and their actions are often estranged. It is frustrating to see families make the same mistakes and mismanagement of transferred assets in my community. Mismanagement has led to us constantly starting over after every generation as we run in this race from behind, trying to catch up!

Depending on which study you read (and there are many), you will get a different picture of the state of Black America. I recommend that you visit the National Urban League website and read their annual report. There, you will find a lot of interesting information, some good and some bad. Progress has been made, but transferring generational wealth is still a big problem.

The following is a breakdown from the August 8, 2023, Federal Reserve report:

Between the fourth quarter of 2019 and the first quarter of 2023, the inflation-adjusted wealth of all three groups grew:

— Average Black household wealth increased by 11.3% to $308,000.
— Average Hispanic household wealth increased by 26.3% to $298,000.
— Average white household wealth increased by 6.2% to $1,268,000.

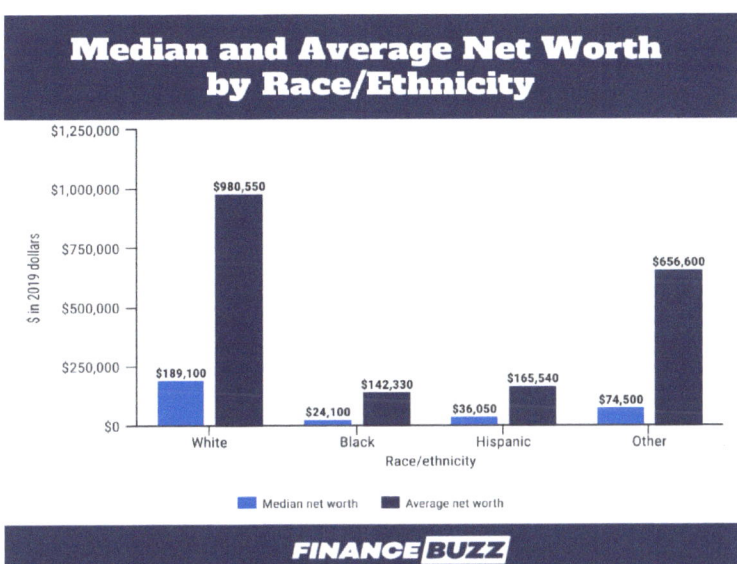

Source: Federal Reserve — Survey of Consumer Finances, 1989 – 2023

Bloomberg published a series called *Black Wealth Transfer, Confronting the Racial Wealth Gap.* (Note: July 26, 2021, www.bloomberg.com)

"The second installment of 'Bloomberg's Power of Difference' series on Black wealth offered a deep dive into issues that impact intergenerational Black wealth transfer. The three-part series, hosted by Bloomberg LP and Bloomberg Philanthropies, seeks to highlight and encourage dialogue about the structures that aid in Black wealth accumulation and extraction.

"Speakers discussed why wealth transfer remains pivotal to building wealth in the United States and explained how the historical lack of opportunity for Black families to preserve and pass on wealth has contributed to the prevalence of racial wealth inequality today.

"Inherited wealth plays a pivotal role in advancing the economic launching point for future generations. Despite the pervasiveness of the American rags to riches story, the wealthiest families have certainly benefited from this capital infusion power—about 30% of the Forbes 400 inherited at least $50 million. Middle and working-class families can use transferred capital and assets to boost emergency savings, make down payments on homes, pay tuition for private schools and higher education, and invest in the financial markets or new entrepreneurship.

"Black families, however, are five times less likely than white families to receive a sizable inheritance. When they do, the amount is still typically three times lower on average than what white families receive. This disparity has contributed to Black Americans falling behind in wealth accumulation while white generational peers are empowered to move towards further economic stability and advancement."

(Please check out the YouTube presentation, *Bloomberg: Power of Difference*).

In my first book, *Wealth: Unlocking the Secrets of Black Family Prosperity and Protection,* I talk about the conditions we face in our community and how comprehensive financial planning could help increase the percentage of Black families building wealth. I also discuss how establishing and maintaining the proper levels of cash reserves and positive cash flows could put a family in the best position to maximize investments in growth accounts, like qualified accounts, brokerage accounts, annuities, and index universal life insurance policies.

We talk about the six components of wealth building:
- Cash Flow management and cash reserves
- Protection planning and debt management
- Investment management
- Tax strategies
- Retirement planning
- Estate planning

Saving, investing, and leveraging wealth with life insurance is the best way to bridge the net worth gap. Having a structured and comprehensive financial plan that addresses every component of wealth building, including generational wealth transfer, is critical in the successful quest to build real wealth. As I always say: **"A journey of a thousand miles starts with one step: planning!"**

My first book, *Wealth: Unlocking the Secrets of Black Family Wealth and Protection*, provided a baseline for understanding the concept of wealth building. The Kindle edition is currently available on Amazon.com. Here is the link: https://a.co/d/i6Gi6yS.

WEALTH

Unlock the secrets to creating and protecting black family prosperity!

"Brilliantly explains wealth strategies. A must-read for every investor."

Arnold S. Goldstein, JD, LLM, Ph.D. Asset Protection Attorney

James L. Marshall, Jr.

xx

As I did in my first book, I will start with a special prayer for you to pray to help receive this information and ask for God's blessings:

My Lord and Savior,

Help me remember, God, that my money, possessions, and riches belong to You. May I use it for Your glory. Keep me from making it the center of my life. Lord, please help me to use the fruits of the spirit in my walk with You. Wisdom, discernment, and understanding are what you gave Solomon, and we are asking for the same. Lord, keep us and guide us because You said if we put You in everything we do, You would direct our paths the right way. We believe and have faith in Your promises. Assist us in keeping a balance in our lives through our faith, family, and finances. We ask these things in the precious name of Jesus. Amen.

Now, if all minds are clear and all hearts are pure, let's begin!

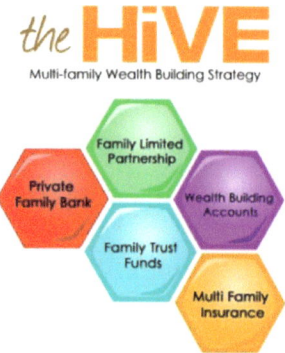

the **HiVE**

Multi-family Wealth Building Strategy

Family Limited Partnership

Private Family Bank

Wealth Building Accounts

Family Trust Funds

Multi Family Insurance

A Journey of a thousand mile starts with one step... **Planning!**

CHAPTER ONE

The Story of George and John Williams

Chapter One

The Story of George and John Williams

John Williams was born in 1920 in a small town in Mississippi. He was a man ahead of his time who understood the importance of planning for future generations. John was taught by his grandfather, George Williams, who was born into slavery the same year Fredrick Douglass published his famous autobiography, ***Narrative of the Life of Fredrick Douglass, an American Slave (written by himself)***. And like Fredrick Douglass, George escaped to freedom and eventually became a successful businessman. His family was believed to be from Ghana, and the Ghanaian way of working hard and strong community ties ran deep in George's blood. George learned from reading any book he could find, as well as listening and talking to those who would listen. He learned that wealth wasn't just about gold, but about the seeds you planted within yourself, seeds that could blossom into a future as bright and hopeful as the dawning sun. And with this hard-earned knowledge he left behind written instructions that stipulated his descendants should use his wealth to build multi-generational wealth. He died in 1895 before he could lay out the steps to accomplish his vision.

After many setbacks brought on by Jim Crowism, racism, and broken promises, John established some financial stability. He rebounded from the devastating setbacks his mother and father were forced to endure because of the social conditions they lived through—setbacks that included the loss of the land Grandfather George left to the family. A generation later, John was starting over from scratch. All he had was an old book his grandfather, George left behind. The book is titled *The Way to Wealth* by Benjamin Franklin. It was written in 1758, but it was still relevant. Knowing that he was turning the same pages that his grandfather had turned gave him all the inspiration and hope he needed to continue toward his goal of building family wealth.

John grew up working in the logging industry and quickly learned the skills of a lumberjack. He was an industrious worker and a natural leader and soon rose through the ranks of the logging company.

In 1945, after several years of working for the logging company, John made a bold decision to start his own business. He saved every penny and bought several acres of land in the woods. Many times, he had to rely on White men to front for him to get the land, but he would not be denied. John built a small sawmill on his land and started cutting and selling lumber.

John's business was successful, but it was not easy. He encountered discrimination from White businesses, who refused to sell him supplies or buy his lumber. He also battled the elements, enduring storms and floods. Despite the challenges, John never gave up. He worked tirelessly to build his business and eventually became one of the most successful lumbermen in Mississippi. He was an inspiration to other Black entrepreneurs and showed that it was possible to achieve success in business despite discrimination and setbacks.

Even with his success in logging, John lived a very modest lifestyle. His family didn't have much money, but John was ambitious. He never forgot his roots and remembered what it was like to grow up with little money. This made him determined to help others in the same situation. John held on to his big dreams for his future and was determined to make them come true.

The Importance of Education

John Williams believed that education was the key to success. He had seen firsthand how education could change lives and was determined to provide his children with the best possible instructions. He was a follower of both Booker T. Washington's views on entrepreneurism and industrial education, as well as W. E. B. Du Bois' belief that civic education with a focus on equal rights was the most important thing for improving life for the Black family. Consequently, he sent his children to good schools and made sure they had tutors to help them with their studies. He also encouraged them to participate in extracurricular activities like sports and clubs. The children did well in school and got good grades. They participated in various activities that made John proud, and he prayed that they would have a bright future.

Investing Wisely

John was a wise investor. He knew that it was important to invest his money prudently, and he took the time to learn about different investment options. Although the information was hard to come by, he persisted in his efforts to educate himself on the concept of making his money work as hard for him as he was working for it! John invested in various assets, including stocks, bonds, and real estate. He also invested in his own business by putting more in than he took out. These investments grew over time, and he built a significant amount of wealth. His efforts did not go unnoticed by his children. From his examples, they learned the importance of investing wisely and started investing their own money when they were young. John's children were well positioned for financial success in the future.

Passing on the Legacy

John was committed to passing on his legacy to his

children. He wanted them to have the same opportunities he had and be successful in life. So, in addition to education, he talked to them about investing and giving back to the community. He also taught them about his own values and beliefs.

The Future of the Williams Family

The Williams family was excited about the future. They believed they could build a lasting legacy that would benefit the family for generations. John and his wife, Cora, were optimistic about the future because their children were all intelligent, motivated, well educated, and had a strong work ethic. As John taught, they were also committed to giving back to the community. This family was confident it could achieve its goals by remaining close-knit and united by a common vision.

The Power of Family History

John Williams was a man whose mission was to build a lasting legacy for his family, and he was determined to do whatever it took to make that happen. One thing that helped John stay focused on his goal was researching his family tree. He learned about his ancestors and their accomplishments, and their stories inspired him. He saw how they overcame challenges and built successful lives and knew he could do the same. His family history gave him a sense of purpose. John knew he was part of a lengthy line of successful people who came from horrible circumstances. This motivated him to keep working hard and building his wealth. He also realized from researching his family history, that it is not what you make, but what you keep that makes the difference.

John remembered, as George did, the stories about his family history going back to Ghana. These stories, told to him by his elders, helped him identify his values and those important to his ancestors. He made sure to incorporate those values into his own life and work toward his goals of building multi-generational wealth.

CHAPTER TWO

Along Came Mary!

SCAN HERE

Chapter Two

Along Came Mary!

A young woman named Mary sat at the kitchen table looking at a document she had read many times over the years. She is the great-great-granddaughter of George Williams, who died in 1895, 30 years after the abolishment of slavery. Mary came across his name and the accompanying documents while researching her family history. She was proud that her great-great-grandfather had escaped to freedom and eventually became a successful businessman. He left behind a handwritten will that stipulated that his descendants should use his wealth to build multi-generational wealth.

Mary is reading the will for the third time.

She is excited to have this important piece of her family's history in her possession. She is very honored to have the opportunity to continue George's legacy, but the challenge also daunts her. It had been twenty years since she came across George's will, and even though Mary was educated and motivated, life and procrastination got the best of her. She has not been able to put anything in place to advance the baton for future generations. But this time will be different!

A year later, Mary sits in her living room, surrounded by her family. As she does every year, she tells them stories about George and his legacy. This time, she is well prepared for her family reunion. This year's theme is **Embrace the Past While Committing to the Future.** She spent a lot of time creating charts, graphs, and biographies of the family elders to include in her official family journal. Mary tells them, "George was a remarkable man who had a dream for his descendants, and we are here today because he existed." The family is all smiles and proud of their heritage. They are committed to carrying on George's legacy.

Mary continues to share, "We can achieve anything we set our minds to. We are strong, we are resilient, and we are together!" Mary reminds them that one of the things that helped them to build family wealth was life insurance. She tells them that her grandfather, John Williams, George's grandson, was the first person in their family to use life insurance to increase wealth. He took out a policy on himself. When he died, the money from the policy went to her mother, who used that money to start her own business. However, her siblings did not use their portion of the inheritance to further the family's wealth, and the family continued to take two steps forward and one step back for years. The assets were not protected from outside influences, bad decisions, or ill-advised investments. "We have got to find a way to stop starting over with every generation!"

Then Mary gave her family the most startling news: "We have already lost the opportunity to have approximately $7,500,000 in family wealth. When George died, he left $5,000 and some land to his family. If that $5,000 had been invested in a conservative account averaging 4% per year, with each generation contributing just $100,000 every 30 years, that family account would be worth $7,500,000 today!

"If you always do what you have always done, you will always get what you have always gotten."

Mary's family journal and extra efforts paid off, and a year later, at the annual family gathering, Mary's grandchildren asked if they could make a presentation to the whole family. Since Mary was the family matriarch, she informed everyone that Malik and Layla wanted to talk to them about something. The family gathered in the living room. They were all excited to hear what Malik and Layla had to say.

Malik said, "Thank you, Grandma. We've been thinking about how we can build on our family's legacy. We believe that one way to do that is to establish a Family Cooperative Trust and private bank."

Layla commented, "A Family Cooperative Trust and private bank would allow us to pool our income and assets and give us more control over our financial future. We could use the private bank to invest in businesses owned by African Americans and provide loans to other family members."

Then Layla gave the following examples of how to use the income generated by the assets owned by the trust to pay for important things like:

- Financial advisors
- CPAs
- Attorneys
- Therapists
- Family doctors and other healthcare providers
- Health insurance premiums
- Life insurance premiums
- Long-term care insurance premiums
- Monthly stipends to qualified family members
- Systematic saving & investing plans.

Layla wrapped up by giving the family this revelation, "Establishing a trust account to own this cooperative or family bank is the key to sustaining and growing our family's wealth for generations to come. Just imagine the possibilities! If we take that same $7,500,000 that Grandma Mary said, we should have had in our family from our great-great-grandfather George's initial $5,000 bequeath and take that forward another 100 years (approximately three generations). If each generation contributed $1,000,000 in life insurance proceeds every 30 years, the family trust would be worth more than $400,000,000, earning just 4% **(providing that earnings in the account were reinvested and no funds were taken out of the accounts).** That's life-changing money that could provide perpetual wealth for our family!"

Mary proudly told her grandchildren, "Impressive idea, Malik and Layla! I think we must find ways to protect our wealth and use it to benefit our community. But how?"

They responded, "We met with a financial advisor named James Marshall, and he told us about a system he developed called *The Hive Family Wealth-building Strategy®,* and he explained to us the theory behind his multi-generational wealth system. Once we reviewed the brochure, it was obvious that this is the right strategy for our family and our wealth-building efforts."

After the family discussed Malik and Layla's proposal, everyone was enthusiastic about the idea of establishing a family Hive. Mary told the family she thought they should move forward with the proposal and called a meeting with the family elders to make up the board of directors and start working on the details.

The family was excited about their future. They are confident they could build a solid and prosperous future for their family by establishing a cooperative and private bank. Mary's bold steps to activate her ancestor's legacy proceeded to move the family to the next stage. This was something John knew many years ago. Now, it's time to share the many benefits of building multi-generational wealth with this generation.

CHAPTER THREE

How To Build Multi-Generational Wealth

SCAN HERE

Chapter Three

How To Build Multi-Generational Wealth

When I met Malik and Layla, they told me about their grandmother, Mary, who shared stories of the financial successes of George and John Williams. They expressed their commitment to carrying on George's legacy. As a financial advisor, I was delighted to work with these young adults and educate them on building multi-generational wealth.

In my own family tree, there were very few entrepreneurs (four, counting myself); however, there is a history of self-reliance and financial improvement from one generation to the next. However, this is not wealth transference. The increase in financial status was based on better opportunities and education—not land, stocks, or businesses transferred to the next generation.

It is not unusual for some family members to have an individualistic approach toward building wealth. After all, there is a lot of truth to the African Proverb *"If you want to go fast, go alone; if you want to go far, go together."*

I can't help but wonder what my family could have achieved if there had been a concentrated effort by multiple family members to acquire land and other investments in a family trust to benefit generations to come. I have realized that the "I got mine, you get yours" mentality that was present in my family still exists. However, efforts are underway to change that.

What about you and your family? Are you aware of the ongoing hindrances that are standing in the way of establishing a multi-generational wealth-building strategy? As Malik and Layla said to their family, I introduced them to the system I developed called the Hive. But before I get into that, let's start with a few tips to build multi-generational wealth.

- **Start early**: The earlier you start saving and investing, the more time your money has to grow. The power of compounded interest is mind blowing!

- **Invest wisely**: Choose investments appropriate for your risk tolerance and time horizon. Invest in companies with strong financial fundamentals instead of hype.

- **Get professional help**: A financial advisor can help create a plan to reach your financial goals and help guide you through turbulent and uncertain times.

- **Instruct your children about money**: Help them develop good financial habits so they can be financially responsible adults. Teach them the mechanics of building wealth. This is not one and done teaching; it must be constant and consistent.

- **Create a family culture of wealth**: Talk to your family about your goals for generational wealth and how they can contribute. Help them to understand the difference between building wealth and living wealthy.

- **Plan for the unexpected**: Make sure you have a plan for what will happen to your wealth if you become incapacitated or pass away. Anticipate and prepare for conditions that can cause losses and put strategies and products in place to address these potential conditions.

The Importance of Financial Education

One of the most important things you can do to build multi-generational wealth is to instruct your children about money. Financial education can help them develop good financial habits and make sound financial decisions throughout their lives.

There are many ways to teach your children about money, starting with talking to them about the value of money and how to save it. Also, teach them about budgeting and making wise financial choices. As they get older, you can teach them about investing and building wealth over time. Many books address financial education for young people; for example, check out my book *Mini Moguls: Lessons in Money Management*.

You can purchase it on Amazon using this link: https://a.co/d/aLhRNhw. This book is designed to instruct children aged nine to 13 about the concepts of financial management. It is written at a sixth-grade reading level and is a very entertaining approach to learning.

Financial education is an essential part of building multi-generational wealth. It can help your children reach their financial goals and create a lasting legacy for your family. Make sure that your children understand and take ownership of the family vision for multi-generational wealth. The education process never ends; the older they get, the more advanced the lessons become. The education process should start as soon as they start asking for money to buy things. When they ask for money, they know it is the only way to get things they want.

John Williams was confident that he had done everything right to provide for his family for generations to come. Still, he did not educate his children about the importance of financial planning, legacy planning, and accumulating and protecting wealth for future generations. More importantly, he did not make sure that his children were committed to the multi-generational wealth vision. **He focused too much on the work and not enough on the plan!** It would take two generations before the vision of George Williams would be rediscovered again! It has been said: *"My great grandfather walked, my grandfather drove an old Ford, my father drove a Cadillac, I drive a Mercedes Benz; my son, he will be walking again. Hard times create strong men, strong men create good times, good times create weak men, and weak men create hard times."*

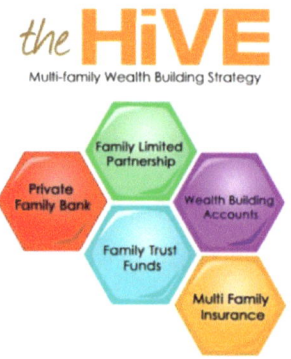

the **HiVE**
Multi-family Wealth Building Strategy

Family Limited Partnership

Private Family Bank

Wealth Building Accounts

Family Trust Funds

Multi Family Insurance

A Journey of a thousand mile starts with one step... **Planning!**

CHAPTER FOUR

What Is the HiVE?

SCAN HERE

Chapter Four

What Is the Hive?

The Hive is a multi-family wealth-building concept that uses family cooperatives, family banks, trust-owned life insurance, and accumulation accounts to advance family wealth through multiple generations. It can be established and funded by individual family members, extended family members, or friends. It uses the concept of cooperative economics to leverage the members' relationships by combining their limited resources to create a larger pool of funds for investment. Tony Robbins explains the concept of personal leverage this way: ***"When you surround yourself with the right people and use those connections to get things done, you're using the power of leverage in the best possible way."***

The Hive is the instrument that powers a family wealth-building movement. It utilizes the collective knowledge, energy, and resources of a close group of people to accomplish their common goal of building multi-generation wealth.

the **HiVE**
Multi-family Wealth Building Strategy ®

MULTI-GENERATIONAL WEALTH
BUILDING STRATEGY

A Family Wealth

This is a multi-family wealth building concept that uses family cooperatives, family banks, trust owned life insurance and accumulation accounts to advance family wealth through multiple generations.

JAMES L. MARSHALL, JR

What Are the Components of the Hive?

Before I explain the components of the multi-generational wealth-building hive, you need to know and understand the components of a natural beehive. The main components of a natural hive are as follows:

Hollow cavity: The hive is typically found in a hollow tree, rock cavity, or other natural cavity. The cavity provides a safe and secure place for the bees to live and work.

Honeycomb: The bees built their honeycombs inside the cavity. The honeycombs are made of wax and provide a place for the bees to store the honey, pollen, and eggs.

Queen cell: The queen cell is a special type of cell bees build to house the queen bee. It is larger than the other cells and is located in the center of the hive.

Brood chamber: The brood chamber is the hive area where the bees raise their young. It is usually located at the bottom of the hive.

Honey super: The honey is the top part of the hive where the bees store honey. The honey super is usually made of a lighter material than the brood chamber, making it easier for the bees to move.

The beehive structure is solid. The honeycombs are made of beeswax, which is an extraordinarily resilient material. The bees build the honeycombs in a hexagonal shape, which is the most efficient way to use the space and create a durable structure. The bees also use their wings to fan the air inside the hive, which helps to keep the hive cool and prevents the honeycombs from melting.

A full beehive can weigh up to 300 pounds and withstand a lot of weight and pressure. The bees defend their hive from predators such as bears, skunks, and raccoons.

Two of the most critical concepts of hive success are communication and hive maintenance.

Communication–Bees communicate with each other through a dance known as the "waggle dance." This dance conveys information about the location of food sources to other worker bees.

Hive Maintenance–Worker bees perform tasks to maintain and clean the hive, removing debris and dead bees to maintain a healthy living environment.

These are just some key aspects of a hive's inner workings. Honeybees exhibit highly organized and cooperative behavior, working together for the survival and prosperity of the colony.

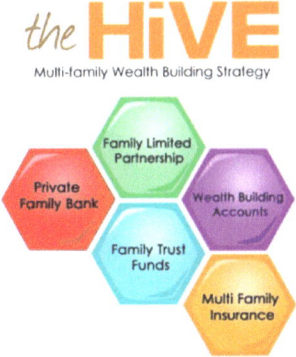

the **HiVE**
Multi-family Wealth Building Strategy

Family Limited Partnership

Private Family Bank

Wealth Building Accounts

Family Trust Funds

Multi Family Insurance

A Journey of a thousand mile starts with one step... **Planning!**

The structure of the Hive: The family wealth-building system is modeled after the concept of the natural beehive and the structure of its colonies.

- **Protect the elderly.**
- **Cultivate the youth.**
- **Secure the assets.**
- **Work together for the benefit and survival of the family.**

Like the beehive, the key component of the family hive is its physical structure, which encourages, supports, and grows cooperative economics.

What is the Corporate Governance or Structure of Your Hive?

Your Hive or organization must have a system of rules, practices, and processes by which it is directed and controlled. Governance exists to protect the interests of all the members and stakeholders. In the case of the "Hive," it protects the interests of those members yet to be born!

Investopedia puts it like this: "Since corporate governance provides the framework for attaining a company's objectives, it encompasses practically every sphere of management, from action plans and internal controls to performance measurements and corporate disclosure."

KEY TAKEAWAYS

- Corporate governance is the structure of rules, practices, and processes used to direct and manage a company.

- A company's board of directors is the primary force influencing corporate governance.

- Bad corporate governance can doubt a company's operations and ultimate profitability.

- Corporate governance covers the areas of environmental awareness, ethical behavior, corporate strategy, compensation, and risk management.

- The basic principles of corporate governance are accountability, transparency, fairness, responsibility, and risk management.

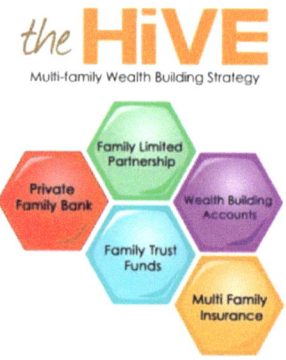

the HiVE

Multi-family Wealth Building Strategy

Family Limited Partnership

Private Family Bank

Wealth Building Accounts

Family Trust Funds

Multi Family Insurance

A Journey of a thousand mile starts with one step... **Planning!**

CHAPTER FIVE

Understanding Corporate Governance

SCAN HERE

Chapter Five

Understanding Corporate Governance

Governance refers specifically to the set of rules, controls, policies, and resolutions put in place to direct corporate behavior. A board of directors is a pivotal governance. Proxy advisors and shareholders are important stakeholders who can affect governance. Communicating a firm's corporate governance is a key component of community and investor relations. For instance, Apple Inc.'s investor relations site outlines its corporate leadership (executive team and board of directors). It provides corporate governance information, including committee charters and governance documents such as bylaws, stock ownership guidelines, and articles of incorporation.

Most companies strive to have exceptional corporate governance. For many shareholders, merely being profitable is not enough. A company must also demonstrate good corporate citizenship through environmental awareness, ethical behavior, and sound corporate governance practices.

Benefits of Corporate Governance

- Good corporate governance creates transparent rules and controls, guides leadership, and aligns the interests of shareholders, directors, management, and employees.

- It helps build trust with investors, the community, and public officials.

- Corporate governance can give investors and stakeholders a clear idea of the company's direction and business integrity.

- It promotes long-term financial viability, opportunity, and returns.

- It can facilitate the raising of capital.

- Good corporate governance can translate to rising share prices.

- It can lessen the potential for economic loss, waste, risk, and corruption.

- It is a game plan for resilience and long-term success.

Corporate Governance and the Board of Directors

The board of directors is the primary direct stakeholder influencing corporate governance. Directors are elected by shareholders or appointed by other board members. They represent the shareholders of the company.

The board is tasked with making important decisions, such as when shareholder resolutions call for prioritizing certain social or environmental concerns.

Boards are often made up of insiders and independent members. Insiders are major shareholders, founders, and executives. Independent directors do not share the ties that insiders have. They are chosen for their experience managing or directing other large companies. Independents are considered helpful for governance because they dilute the concentration of power and help align shareholder interests with those of the insiders.

The board of directors must ensure the company's corporate governance policies, corporate strategy, risk management, accountability, transparency, and ethical business practices.

A board of directors should consist of diverse individuals, including those with skills and knowledge of the business and those who can bring a fresh perspective from outside the company and industry.

The Principles of Corporate Governance

While there can be many principles that a company believes make sense, some of the more well known include the following:

- Fairness

The board of directors must treat shareholders, employees, vendors, and communities fairly and with equal consideration.

- Transparency
The board should provide shareholders and other stakeholders with timely, accurate, and clear information about financial performance, conflicts of interest, and risks.

- Risk Management
The board and management must determine risks of all kinds and how best to control them. They must act on those recommendations to manage them. They must inform all relevant parties about the existence and status of risks.

- Responsibility
The board is responsible for overseeing corporate matters and management activities. It must be aware of and support the company's successful, ongoing performance. Part of its responsibility is to recruit and hire a CEO. The board must act in the best interests of the company and its investors.

- Accountability

  The board must explain the purposes of a company's activities and the results of its conduct. It and company leadership are accountable for assessing a company's capacity, potential, and performance. It must communicate issues of importance to shareholders.

How to Assess Corporate Governance

As an investor, you want to select companies that practice good corporate governance to avoid losses and negative consequences like bankruptcy.

You can research certain areas of a company to determine whether it's practicing good corporate governance. These areas include the following:

- Disclosure practices

- Executive compensation structure (whether it's tied only to performance or also to other metrics)

- Risk management (the checks and balances on decision-making)

- Policies and procedures for reconciling conflicts of interest (how the company approaches business decisions that might conflict with its mission statement)

- The members of the board of directors (their stake in profits or conflicting interests)

- Contractual and social obligations (how a company approaches areas such as climate change)

- Relationship with vendors

- Complaints received from shareholders and how they were addressed

- Audits (the frequency of internal and external audits and how issues have been overseen)

Types of Bad Governance Practices

- Companies that do not cooperate sufficiently with auditors or do not select auditors with the appropriate scale, resulting in the publication of spurious or noncompliant financial documents.

- Bad executive compensation packages fail to create an optimal incentive for corporate officers.

- Poorly structured boards make it too difficult for shareholders to oust effective incumbents.

- Be sure to include corporate governance in your due diligence before making an investment decision.

What Are the 4 Ps of Corporate Governance?

The four P's of corporate governance are as follows:

1. People

2. Process

3. Performance

4. Purpose

Why Is Corporate Governance Important?

Corporate governance is important because it creates a system of rules and practices that determines how a company operates and how it aligns with the interests of all its stakeholders. Good corporate governance leads to ethical business practices, which lead to financial viability, which can, in turn, attract investors.

What Are the Basic Principles of Corporate Governance?

The basic principles of corporate governance are accountability, transparency, fairness, responsibility, and risk management.

The Bottom Line

Corporate governance consists of the guiding principles a company establishes to direct all of its operations, from compensation, risk management, and employee treatment to reporting unfair practices, dealing with the impact on the climate, and more.

.

Corporate governance that calls for upstanding, transparent company behavior leads a company to make ethical decisions that benefit its stakeholders. It can underscore a potential investment for investors. Bad corporate governance leads to a company's breakdown, often resulting in scandals and bankruptcy.

I realize this seems to be a lot of information; however, understanding and using corporate governance as a guideline when setting up your family Hive is a prudent approach to creating and maintaining a solid and effective entity. **This structure provides an opportunity for "the Hive" to be perpetual.**

Structure, process, and the use of proper legal documents turn this diagram into a working system.

How **the HiVE** works

CHAPTER SIX

How To Get Started

SCAN HERE

Chapter Six

How to Get Started

The first step is to get commitment from family members who want to participate, and take an assessment of your assets.

Next, gather a list of all the assets you want to include in the family Hive (Cooperative Trust); include your bank accounts, retirement accounts, life insurance policies, real estate, and other valuables. This will help you understand what you are working with and make informed decisions about transferring your wealth.

1. Consider your goals. What are your goals for transferring your wealth? How much should go to individual family members, and how much should go to the Cooperative Trust?

2. Do you want to provide for the next or multiple generations? What financial resources do you

want to provide for family members, young and old? What are your charitable aspirations for the family Hive? Once you know your goals, you can develop a plan to achieve them.

3. Talk to a financial advisor, tax consultant, and an estate planning attorney.

4. A financial advisor can help you develop a plan that meets your needs and goals. The estate planning attorney and tax consultant can help you to understand the legal and tax implications of transferring your wealth.

5. Complete a comprehensive financial plan and share it with all the members of the Hive. Make sure that everyone understands the plan, and that all of their questions and concerns are addressed.

6. It's essential that everyone involved understands the goals, strategies, and structure of the family Hive. The objectives and structure should be clearly communicated in all legal documents governing the Hive. It is also important that every

adult family member completes his/her financial plan as well as the family Hive financial plan.

7. Review your plan periodically.

8. Your circumstances and goals may change over time, so it's important to review your plan periodically and make changes as needed. These reviews should occur during quarterly meetings with your family's executive committee.

9. The executive committee should include the board chairman or president, executive director, treasurer, and secretary.

10. Establish the structure of your family Hive.

The best approach is to mimic the leadership structure of a nonprofit organization. These organizations typically consist of three main levels. Here is a chart of a nonprofit organization leadership chart:

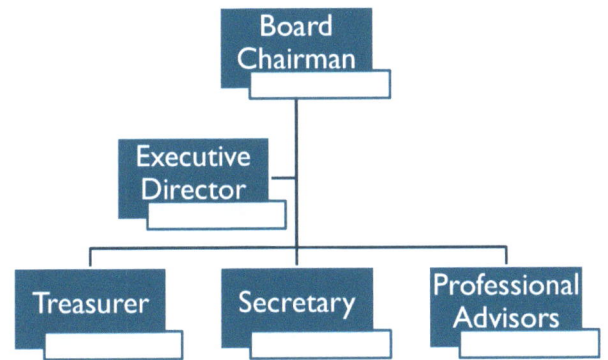

Board of Directors: This group sets the mission, vision, and goals, oversees finances, and approves the budget. It meets monthly or quarterly.

Executive Director or Chief Executive Officer: This person is responsible for day-to-day operations, implementing board decisions, and reports to the board of directors.

Program Director (Responsible for programs and services): Develops and implements programs that meet the organization's mission and goals. Works with staff. Meets with the board of directors.

Finance Director or Treasurer (Responsible for finances): Oversees budget, accounting, and financial reporting. Works with staff. Meets with the board of directors.

Other Staff: may include fundraising coordinators, program coordinators, administrative assistants, and volunteers. They support the organization's work in numerous ways.

The chart shows the various levels of leadership and their respective roles and responsibilities. It can help you understand how the organization is run and who is responsible for what.

It is important to note that a nonprofit organization's leadership chart may vary depending on its size and complexity. Smaller organizations may have a simpler chart, while larger organizations may have a more complex chart.

Board of Directors: *4-year term* — The board of directors is responsible for the organization's overall governance. They see the organization's mission and vision and approve its budget. And oversee its financial performance. The board typically consists of a mix of volunteers and professionals with expertise in finance, law, marketing, and fundraising.

Executive Director: *4-year term* — The executive director is the organization's chief executive officer. They are responsible for the organization's day-to-day operations and ensuring it meets its goals. The executive director typically reports to the board of directors.

Program Staff: *(Treasurer and Secretary) 2-year term* — The program staff is responsible for delivering the organization's programs and services. They may be responsible for fundraising and marketing: research, advocacy, or direct service delivery. The program staff typically reports to the executive director.

In addition to these three main levels above, a

nonprofit organization may have other levels of management, such as a management team or a departmental structure. The specific structure of a nonprofit organization will vary depending on its size, complexity, and funding sources. Here are some of the factors that should be considered when designing a nonprofit organization's leadership structure:

The Size and Complexity of the Organization

The structure of a nonprofit organization **must be flexible enough to accommodate its size and complexity**. For example, a small nonprofit organization may have a simple structure with a few key decision-makers, while a large nonprofit organization may have a more complex structure with multiple levels of management.

The Nature of the Organization's Work

The structure of a nonprofit organization will also need to be aligned with the nature of the organization's work. For example, an organization that provides direct service delivery may need a more decentralized structure with decision-making authority at the program level, while an organization that engages in advocacy may need a more centralized structure with decision-making authority at the executive level.

The Organization's Funding Sources

The structure of a nonprofit organization may also be influenced by its funding sources.
For example, an organization that receives government funding may be required to have a certain level of board involvement, while an organization that receives foundation funding may be required to have a more professionalized management structure.

The leadership structure of a nonprofit organization is an integral part of its overall success. By carefully considering the factors unique to each organization, nonprofit leaders can design a structure to help the organization achieve its goals. The family Hive should be led by a board of directors and lead by an executive committee.

Here are some additional resources that you may find helpful:

- The American College of Trust and Estate Counsel: https://www.actec.org/

- The National Association of Estate Planners & Councils: https://www.naepc.org/

- The Society of Trust and Estate Practitioners: https://www.step.org/

- The American Bar Association: https://www.americanbar.org/

CHAPTER SEVEN

Ten Things to Consider as You Set Up Your Family Hive

SCAN HERE

Chapter Seven

Ten Things to Consider as You Set Up Your Family Hive

1. **Name beneficiaries and contingent beneficiaries on your assets.**

   This is the simplest way to transfer your wealth to your heirs. When you name beneficiaries on your assets, such as your bank accounts, retirement accounts, and life insurance policies, they will automatically receive those assets upon your death. It is important to make clear which assets you want to go to your heirs and which assets you want to go to the family trust.

2. **Create a will.**

   A will is a legal document that specifies how you want your assets to be distributed after your death. You can use a will to leave specific assets to specific people or create a more general plan for how your assets should be distributed. Each adult member of the family should have a will.

3. **Set up a trust.**

A trust is a legal entity that holds assets for the benefit of another person or entity. Trusts can protect assets from creditors, provide for minors or disabled beneficiaries, or minimize estate taxes. Trusts are the most important document used to assure perpetual wealth transfer over multiple generations!

4. **Make annual gifts.**

In 2024 you can give up to $18,000 per person per year to each of your heirs without incurring gift taxes. This is a wonderful way to transfer wealth to your heirs while you're still alive and also help reduce your asset taxes.

5. **Borrow money from your heirs.**

If you need cash, you can borrow money from your heirs. This can be an excellent way to transfer wealth to your heirs while providing them with a steady income stream.

6. **Start a family business.**

If you own a business, you can transfer ownership of the business to your heirs. This can be a fantastic way to keep the business in the family and to provide your heirs with a source of income. This becomes particularly important if you decide to take your business public. Holding voting shares in the family trust can help the family maintain control of the publicly traded company for years.

7. **Provide financial education.**

One of the best ways to help your heirs manage their wealth is to provide them with financial education. This includes teaching them about budgeting, investing, and saving. We recommend retaining the help of professional and specific age-appropriate teaching materials in this endeavor; consider the following resources:

- *Mini Moguls: Lessons in Money Management*

- Dallas Federal Reserve wealth education material

8. **Communicate your wishes.**

It's essential to communicate your wishes about your wealth to your heirs. This will help them understand your intentions and make decisions about your assets after your death. The best way to accomplish this is with a comprehensive financial plan, which should be used for all adult family members.

9. **Get professional help.**

If you're unsure how to transfer your wealth to the next generation, getting professional help is a good idea. A financial advisor or estate planning attorney can help you create a plan that meets your specific needs. This relationship should be ongoing throughout the journey.

10. **Purchase and maintain as much life insurance as you can afford!**

These are just a few of the many ways to transfer wealth to the next generation. The best way to transfer your wealth will depend on your circumstances and goals. It's important to talk to a financial advisor or estate planning attorney to get personalized advice.

CHAPTER EIGHT

Trusts to Consider for Multi-Generational Wealth Transfer

SCAN HERE

Chapter Eight

Trust to Consider for Multi-Generational Wealth Transfer

A few distinct types of trusts can be used to assure multi-generational wealth transfer. Here are a few of the most common.

Dynasty trusts are designed to last for many generations. They are often funded with life insurance proceeds, which can help to grow the trust's assets over time. Dynasty trusts can provide great flexibility for the grantor, as they can be used to control how the trust assets are distributed and managed.

Generation-skipping trusts (GSTs) are irrevocable trusts that allow the grantor to transfer assets to their grandchildren or great-grandchildren without incurring gift or estate taxes. This can help to preserve multi-generational wealth by reducing the amount of taxes that are paid on the transfer assets.

Spendthrift trusts are designed to protect trust assets from creditors and other creditors. This can be important for safeguarding multi-generational wealth, as it can help to ensure that the trust assets are not lost due to the financial problems of a beneficiary.

Charitable trusts can support a charitable cause while also benefiting family members. This can be a good option for families who want to give back to the community and ensure their wealth is used for good.

The best type of trust for ensuring multi-generational wealth will vary depending on the family's specific needs and circumstances. It is important to consult with an estate planning attorney to discuss your options and create a trust tailored to your needs.

Here are some additional factors to consider when choosing a trust for multi-generational wealth:

- **The size of the estate.** A dynasty trust may be the best option if the estate is large. However, a GST or a spendthrift trust may be a better fit if the estate is smaller.

- **The age of the beneficiaries.** If the beneficiaries are young, a trust with a longer term may be necessary to protect the assets until they are mature enough to manage them.

- **The goals of the family.** What are the family's goals for the trust? Do they want to preserve wealth for future generations? Do they want to use the trust to support a charitable cause?

Once you have considered these factors, you can work with an estate planning attorney to choose the right of trust for your family.

Sample of a Dynasty Trust

This Trust Agreement (the "Trust Agreement") is made and entered into as of the [DATE] by and between [GRANTOR], a [STATE] resident (the "Grantor").

WHEREAS, the Grantor desires to create a trust for the benefit of his/her family and descendants and

WHEREAS, the Grantor desires to use life insurance to fund the trust and to grow the trust's assets over time.

NOW, THEREFORE, for a good and valuable consideration, the receipt and sufficiency of which is hereby acknowledged, the Grantor does hereby establish and create the [TRUST NAME], which shall be governed by the following terms and conditions:

1. **Trust Purpose**. The purpose of the Trust is to provide for the benefit of the Grantor's family and descendants in perpetuity.

2. **Trust Property**. The Trust shall initially be funded with the following assets:

   *The Proceeds of a life insurance policy on the life of the Grantor; and
   *Any other assets that the Grantor may subsequently transfer to the Trust.

3. **Trust Beneficiaries**. The initial beneficiaries of the trust shall be the Grantor's children, Grandchildren, and great-grandchildren. The trust shall continue for the benefit of the Grantor of the Grantor's descendants in perpetuity.

4. **Trust Distributions**. The Trustee shall distribute the income and principal if the Trust

to the beneficiaries in accordance with the following terms:

* The Trustee shall pay to each beneficiary as annual income equal to [PERCENTAGE] of the value of the Trust assets.

* The Trustee may also make additional distributions to the beneficiaries at the Trustee's discretion.

* The Trustee shall not distribute any principal to the beneficiaries until death of the last surviving beneficiary of the Grantor's generation.

5. **Trustee **. The initial Trustee of the Trust shall be [TRUSTEE NAME]. The Grantor may, at any time, appoint a successor trustee.

6. **Trust Protector**. The Grantor appoints [TRUST PROTECTOR NAME] as the Trust Protector. The Trust Protector shall have the power to do the following:

*Remove and appoint a trustee.

*Amend the terms of the Trust; and

*Take any other action that the Trust Protector deems necessary to protect the interest of the beneficiaries.

7. **Administration **. The Trustee shall administer the Trust in accordance with the terms of this Trust Agreement and applicable law. The Trustee shall have all the powers and discretion necessary to manage and invest the Trust assets.

8. **Termination **. The Trust shall terminate upon the death of the last surviving beneficiary of the Grantor's generation. Upon termination, the remaining Trust assets be distributed to the Grantor's heirs at law.

9. IN WITNESS WHEREOF, the Grantor has executed this Trust Agreement as of the date first written above.

[GRANTOR

***

This is just a sample dynasty trust. It is important to consult with an estate planning attorney to create a trust tailored to your specific needs and circumstances.

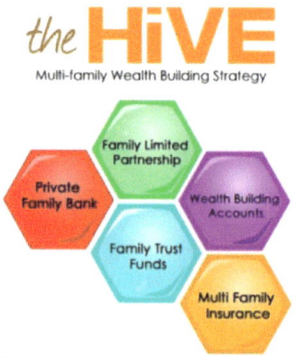

the **HiVE**
Multi-family Wealth Building Strategy

Family Limited Partnership

Private Family Bank

Wealth Building Accounts

Family Trust Funds

Multi Family Insurance

A Journey of a thousand mile starts with one step... **Planning!**

CHAPTER NINE

The Benefits of a Multi-Generational Wealth Plan

SCAN HERE

Chapter Nine

The Benefits of a Multi-Generational Wealth Plan

- **Security and stability**: Multi-generational wealth can provide a sense of security and stability for future generations. It can help them to weather financial storms and unexpected events.

- **Legacy**: Multi-generational wealth can create a lasting legacy for your family. It can be used to promote charitable giving and other philanthropic activities.

- **Opportunity**: Multi-generational wealth can allow future generations to pursue their dreams and achieve their goals. It can help them to get a good education, start a business, or buy a home.

- **The challenges of multi-generational wealth:** While there are many benefits to building multi-generational wealth, there are also some challenges. Here are a few of the most familiar challenges:

- ✓ **Long-term perspective.** Building multi-generational wealth requires a long-term perspective. It takes time to accumulate wealth and ensure that it is managed and invested wisely.

- ✓ **Risk.** Multi-generational wealth is vulnerable to unforeseen events like economic downturns or family disputes.

- **Responsibility:** Building multi-generational wealth comes with a great deal of responsibility. You must carefully manage your wealth wisely and ensure it is used for good.

Like any system built to last, a family hive is only as strong as its parts—and by parts, I mean members. The secret to a strong family hive is making sure that every family unit has its own financial plan, life insurance policies, and estate plans. The families should enrich the hive; the Hive should supplement the riches of the families.

Frequently Asked Questions Regarding Estate Planning

What is estate planning?

Estate planning is the process of making decisions about your assets and how you want them to be distributed after your death. It can also involve planning for your healthcare and financial affairs if you become incapacitated.

Why do I need an estate plan?

There are many reasons why you should have an estate plan. Here are a few:

- To ensure that your assets are distributed according to your wishes.

- To avoid probate, which is the court-supervised process of distributing your assets after your death.

- To protect your assets from creditors and lawsuits.

- To provide for your loved ones if you become incapacitated.

- To minimize estate taxes.

What documents are included in an estate plan?

The specific documents included in your estate plan will vary depending on your individual circumstances. However, some common documents include:

- A will: A will is a legal document that states who you want to inherit your assets and how you want them to be distributed.

- A living will: A living will is a legal document that states your wishes for end-of-life care, such as whether you want to be kept on life support.

- A durable power of attorney: A durable power of attorney is a legal document that appoints someone to make financial decisions for you if you become incapacitated.

- A health care proxy: A health care proxy is a legal document that appoints someone to make healthcare decisions for you if you become incapacitated.

What happens if I don't have an estate plan?

If you don't have an estate plan, your assets will be distributed according to the laws of your state. This may not be what you want, and it could result in your assets being distributed to people you don't want or in a way that is not in your best interests.

Whom should I talk to about estate planning?

You should talk to a financial advisor and an attorney specializing in estate planning. They can help you understand your options and create an estate plan that meets your individual needs.

Here are some additional questions that you may have about estate planning:

How much does estate planning cost?

The cost of estate planning will vary depending on the complexity of your situation and the attorney you choose. However, it is generally a worthwhile investment to protect your assets and ensure that your wishes are carried out after your death.

How often should I update my estate plan?

Your estate plan should be reviewed and updated periodically, especially if there are major changes in your life, such as marriage, divorce, the birth of a child, or the death of a loved one.

What are some of the challenges of estate planning?

One of the biggest challenges of estate planning is facing one's mortality. It can be difficult to think about what will happen after one dies, but it is important to do so to ensure that one's wishes are carried out.

Another challenge of estate planning is dealing with the emotions of your loved ones. You may want to ensure that your assets are distributed in a fair and equitable way, but you also need to be sensitive to the feelings of your loved ones.

What are some of the benefits of estate planning?

There are many benefits to estate planning. Here are a few:

- Peace of mind: Knowing that your affairs are in order can give you peace of mind, knowing that your loved ones will be cared for after you die.

- Control: Estate planning gives you control over how your assets are distributed after your death.

- Flexibility: Estate planning can be flexible and can be updated as your needs change.

- Savings: Estate planning can help you save

money on taxes.

If you are considering estate planning, it is essential to research and talk to an attorney who can help you create an estate plan that meets your needs.

CHAPTER TEN

Are You Ready to Start Building Multi-Generational Wealth?

SCAN HERE

Chapter Ten

Are you ready to start building multi-generational wealth?

Building multi-generational wealth is a challenging but rewarding goal. It takes time, effort, and a long-term perspective. These are not attributes that everyone in the family possesses. However, the benefits of multi-generational wealth can be significant. It can provide security, stability, and opportunity for future generations. It can also create a lasting legacy for your family.

It is important that you start where you are and grow from there. Keep talking about the goals and action steps to your family members and when they are ready to participate, bring them in slowly; but educate them quickly.

The secret to a successful multi-generational wealth building strategy is comprehensive financial planning, but the most important vehicle to building and transferring multi-generational wealth is life insurance!

Life insurance provides financial protection for your loved ones after you pass away. It can be used to fund your Family Cooperative Trust or Hive, as well.

There are two main categories of life insurance: term life and permanent life insurance.

Term life insurance is temporary coverage for a specific period, like 10, 20, or 30 years. It's generally cheaper than permanent life insurance because it only pays out if you die within the term. This is a good option if you want to cover things like a mortgage or children's college education during a specific period. Or if your insurance needs are greater than your ability to afford permanent coverage.

Permanent life insurance covers you for your whole life, and typically builds cash value over time. This cash value can be accessed through loans or withdrawals. There are several types of permanent life insurance:

- Whole life insurance offers guaranteed growth on the cash value and a fixed premium.

- Universal life or Fixed Index life insurance has flexible premiums and allows you to invest the cash value in different ways.

- Variable life insurance invests the cash value in the stock market, so the cash value can fluctuate.

For the benefit of multi-generational wealth transfer, the best type of coverage is fixed index life insurance. This type of policy not only allows you to control large sums of money for little investment; but it can also be used to fund the private family bank.
This is accomplished by over-funding the policy up to the modified endowment limit.

A modified endowment contract (MEC) is a cash-value life insurance policy that's lost its preferential tax treatment because it has too much cash value built up too quickly. In simpler terms, the Internal Revenue Service (IRS) considers it more of an investment than life insurance.

Here's how it works:

Tax advantages of life insurance: Normally, cash value builds up in a life insurance policy tax-deferred, and withdrawals from that cash value are typically tax-free up to the amount you've paid in premiums. This is a significant tax benefit.

The "seven-pay test": The IRS has rules to prevent people from using life insurance primarily for tax-advantaged savings instead of life insurance protection. There's a test called the "seven-pay test" that limits how much premium you can pay into a policy in the first seven years to qualify for the full tax benefits.

Becoming an MEC: If you pay too much premium too soon and fail the seven-pay test, your policy becomes an MEC.

Here's what happens when a policy becomes an MEC:

Loses tax benefits: Withdrawals from the cash value are generally taxed as ordinary income, which can be a much higher tax rate than you'd pay on a normal life insurance withdrawal. There may also be tax penalties for early withdrawals.

Death benefit still tax-free: The good news is that the death benefit payout from an MEC is still generally income tax-free for your beneficiaries.

Here are some additional points to consider:

MECs are created by exceeding premium limits, not by taking money out.
There are ways to access some of the cash value from an MEC tax-free, but it's more complex than with a standard policy.

If you're considering a cash-value life insurance policy, it's important to understand the MEC rules and work with a financial advisor to make sure you don't accidentally trigger MEC status.

However, as long as you do not violate the MEC rules, the family will have the ability to pull funds from the policy's cash value income tax free.

Of course, it is important to use good judgment when pulling funds from the policy's cash value. Make sure that the withdrawals are working in partnership with the financial plan. Keep in mind that the greatest benefit of the life insurance policy is the death benefit, and its ability to fund the growth of the Family Cooperative Trust or Hive over multiply generations.

If you are interested in building multi-generational wealth, many resources are available to help you get started. You can talk to a financial advisor, read books and articles on the topic, or join a support group.

Let us start building your family Hive today!

You can contact us at **www.marshallyourmoney.com**. With careful planning and execution, you can create a lasting legacy for your family.

The Williams family will go on to establish a financially strong and emotionally stable family committed to sustaining and growing multi-generational wealth. They will also be able to provide stability in their community through their charitable contributions to organizations dedicated to improving the quality of life in our communities.

So, what are you waiting for? Start establishing your family Hive today!

James Marshall

1404 Lake Pointe Parkway
Sugar Land TX 77478
O 832.410.7233
M 602.727.5728
james@marshallyourmoney.com
www.MarshallYourMoney.com

MARSHALL
Wealth Management, LLC
A Registered Investment Advisory Firm

Use this financial client questionnaire to start organizing your finances and begin the process of building your Family Hive.

You can't map out your journey without first knowing your starting point. Honest self-assessment is a critical first step towards any wealth building strategy.

MARSHALL
WEALTH
MANAGEMENT
-Financial Services
-Financial Planning
-Investment Management
-Life Planning
-Financial Education System

CLIENTQUESTIONNAIRE

Name:

Date:

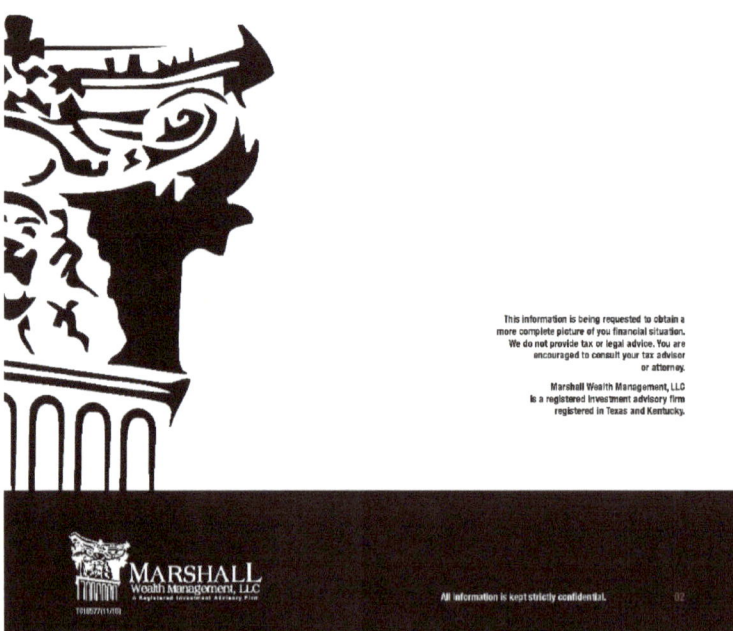

This information is being requested to obtain a
more complete picture of you financial situation.
We do not provide tax or legal advice. You are
encouraged to consult your tax adviser
or attorney.

Marshall Wealth Management, LLC
is a registered investment advisory firm
registered in Texas and Kentucky.

MARSHALL
Wealth Management, LLC
A Registered Investment Advisory Firm

All information is kept strictly confidential.   02

James L. Marshall, Jr. | 92

BACKGROUND - FAMILY DATA

Name (First, Middle Initial, Last)	Date of Birth	Place of Birth	Social Security #
Your Name			
Spouse			
Child			
Child			
Child			
Child			

RESIDENCE

Street Address			
Home Phone		Mobile Phone	
Other			
Home Email			

EMPLOYMENT

Your Occupation	Employer	How Long	Address		Phone
Spouse's Occupation	Employer	How Long	Address		Phone
Your Work Email		Spouse's Work Email			

INCOME

Your Primary Income	Base Salary	Est. Bonus	Est. Commissions	Est. Stock Options
Spouse's Primary Income	Base Salary	Est. Bonus	Est. Commissions	Est. Stock Options

BUSINESS INCOME		**OTHER INCOME**	

1404 Lake Pointe Parkway
Sugar Land, TX 77478
O 832.449.7293
M 502.727.5728
james@marshallyourmoney.com
www.MarshallYourMoney.com

03   All information is kept strictly confidential.

THE HIVE | 93

BUDGET SUMMARY - MONTHLY EXPENSE ITEMS

HOUSING ITEMS	
Groceries/Dining Out	
Mortgage/Rent	
Real Estate Taxes	
House/Renter's Insurance	
Utilities (Electric, Gas, Water)	
Telephone/Cell/Internet	
Housing Repair/Maint/Lawn	
Other Housing	
TRANSPORTATION	
Vehicle Payment/Lease	
Vehicle Insurance	
Vehicle Gas/Fuel	
Vehicle Repair (Oil, Tires, Brakes)	
Other Transportation (Bus/Cab)	
OTHER ITEMS	
Clothing	
Personal Care	
Medical/Dental	
Entertainment	
Alimony/Child Support	
Child Care	
Gifts	
Charity/Tithes	
Debt Maintenance (credit cards)	
Student Loans	
Other Loan Payments	
Other Items	
MONTHLY SAVINGS	
IRA Contributions (Traditional)	
IRA Contributions (Roth)	
Company Retirement Plan	
(401ks, TSP, SEP, etc.)	
Company Matching Contribution	
(percentage)	
Other savings	

All information is kept strictly confidential.

James L. Marshall, Jr. | 94

SAVINGS/INVESTMENTS

Item	Jointly Held	Yourself	Spouse	Children
Savings Account	$	$	$	$
Savings Account	$	$	$	$
Checking Account	$	$	$	$
Certificate of Deposit	$	$	$	$
Money Market Fund	$	$	$	$
IRA	$	$	$	$
Employer Sponsored Retirement Account	$	$	$	$
529 Plan	$	$	$	$
Pension	$	$	$	$
Brokerage Accounts	$	$	$	$
Savings Bonds	$	$	$	$
Annuities	$	$	$	$
Other	$	$	$	$
Other	$	$	$	$
Other	$	$	$	$

1404 Lake Pointe Parkway
Sugar Land, TX 77478
O 882.440.7293
M 502.727.5728
james@marshallyourmoney.com
www.MarshallYourMoney.com

All information is kept strictly confidential.

REAL ESTATE

Property	Purchase Year	Purchase Price	Improvements or Capital Expenditures	Current Estate Market Value
Your Residence				
Second Home				
Rental Property				
Land				

MORTGAGE/EQUITY LINES OF CREDIT

Property	Monthly Payment Principal & Interest Only	Interest Rate	Unpaid Balance
Your Residence			
Second Home			
Rental Property			
Land			

LOANS, DEBT AND PERSONAL PROPERTY

Type of Loan	Monthly Payment	Months Remaining	Unpaid Balance

NOTES

Your Driver's License # _____   Issue Date _____   Expiration Date _____

Your Driver's License # _____   Issue Date _____   Expiration Date _____

All information is kept strictly confidential.

James L. Marshall, Jr. | 96

INSURANCE

Property	Company Name	Amount of Coverage	Annual Premium
Auto Policies			
Home Insurance Policies			
Umbrella Coverage			

INSURANCE COVERAGE - LIFE INSURANCE

Provider Company	Policy Loan	Family Member Insured	Annual Premium	Cash Value	Amount of Coverage

INSURANCE COVERAGE - DISABILITY AND/OR LONG-TERM CARE

Provider Company	Family Member Insured	Annual Premium	Monthly Benefit

NOTES

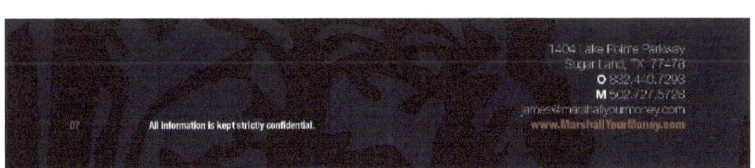

1404 Lake Pointe Parkway
Sugar Land, TX 77478
O 832.440.7299
M 502.727.5728
james@marshallyourmoney.com
www.MarshallYourMoney.com

07   All information is kept strictly confidential.

THE HIVE | 97

ADDITIONAL INFORMATION

Do you have a valid, executed will? (Yes or No)	
Do you have a trust? (Yes or No)	
Do you have an attorney? (Yes or No)	
Do you have an accountant? (Yes or No)	

Goals	Retirement Date	Anticipated Social Security Benefits	Additional Information

NOTES

_____

_____

_____

_____

_____

_____

_____

_____

MARSHALL
Wealth Management, LLC
A Registered Investment Advisory Firm

All information is kept strictly confidential.

James L. Marshall, Jr. | 98

MARSHALL
WEALTH
MANAGEMENT

-Financial Services
-Financial Planning
-Investment Management
-Life Planning
-Financial Education System

RISKTOLERANCEQUESTIONNAIRE

Name:

Circle the response that best describes you. Remember that risk tolerance is largely subjective, so there is no right or wrong answer.

LIFE STAGE

1. **What is your current age?**
a) 65 or older ☐
b) 60 to 64. ☐
c) 55 to 59 ☐
d) 50 to 54 ☐
e) Under 50 ☐

2. **When do you expect to need to withdraw cash from your retirement portfolio?**
a) In less than 1 year ☐
b) Within 1 to 2 years ☐
c) Within 2 to 5 years ☐
d) Within 5 to 10 years ☐
e) Not for at least 10 years ☐

FINANCIAL RESOURCES

3. **How many months of current living expenses could you cover with your present savings and liquid, short-term investments, before you would have to draw on your retirement portfolio?**
a) Less than 3 months ☐
b) 3 to 6 months ☐
c) 6 to 12 months ☐
d) More than 12 months ☐

1404 Lake Pointe Parkway
Sugar Land, TX 77478
O 832-410-7203
M 502.727.5728
james@marshallyourmoney.com
www.MarshallYourMoney.com

09   All information is kept strictly confidential.

FINANCIAL RESOURCES

4. Over the next few years, what do you expect will happen to your income?
a) It will probably decrease substantially. ☐
b) It will probably decrease slightly. ☐
c) It will probably stay the same. ☐
d) It will probably increase slightly. ☐
e) It will probably increase substantially. ☐

5. What percentage of your gross annual income have you been able to save in recent years?
a) None ☐
b) 1 to 5% ☐
c) 5 to 10% ☐
d) 10 to 15% ☐
e) more than 15% ☐

6. Over the next few years, what do you expect will happen to your rate of savings?
a) It will probably decrease substantially. ☐
b) It will probably decrease slightly. ☐
c) It will probably stay the same. ☐
d) It will probably increase slightly. ☐
e) It will probably increase substantially ☐

EMOTIONAL RISK TOLERANCE

7. What are your growth expectations for your portfolio?
a) I don't care if my portfolio keeps pace with inflation; I just want to preserve my capital ☐
b) My growth should keep pace with inflation, with minimum volatility ☐
c) My growth should be slightly more than inflation, with only moderate volatility ☐
d) My growth should significantly exceed inflation, even if this could mean significant volatility ☐

8. How would you characterize your personality?
a) I'm a pessimist. I always expect the worst. ☐
b) I'm anxious. No matter what you say, I'll worry. ☐
c) I'm cautious but open to new ideas. Convince me. ☐
d) I'm objective. Show me the pros and cons and I can make a decision and live with it. ☐
e) I'm optimistic. Things always work out in the end. ☐

9. When monitoring your investments and savings over time, what do you think you will tend to focus on?
a) Individual investments that are doing poorly. ☐
b) Individual investments that are doing very well. ☐
c) The recent results of my overall portfolio. ☐
d) The long term performance of my overall portfolio. ☐

MARSHALL Wealth Management, LLC
a Registered Investment Advisory Firm

All information is kept strictly confidential.

James L. Marshall, Jr. | 100

EMOTIONAL RISK TOLERANCE

10. **Suppose you had $10,000 to place in savings or investments and the choice of 5 different portfolios with a range of possible outcomes after a single year. Which of the following portfolios would you feel most comfortable investing in?**
a) Portfolio A, which could have a balance ranging from $9,900 to $10,300 at the end of the year. ☐
b) Portfolio B, which could have a balance ranging from $9,800 to $10,600 at the end of the year. ☐
c) Portfolio C, which could have a balance ranging from $9,600 to $11,000 at the end of the year. ☐
d) Portfolio D, which could have a balance ranging from $9,200 to $12,200 at the end of the year. ☐
e) Portfolio E, which could have a balance ranging from $8,400 to $14,000 at the end of the year. ☐

11. **If the value of your investment portfolio dropped by 20% in one year, what would you do?**
a) Fire my investment advisor. ☐
b) Move my money to more conservative financial products immediately to reduce the potential for future losses. ☐
c) Monitor the situation, and if it looks like things could continue to deteriorate, move some of my money to more conservative financial products. ☐
d) Consult with my investment advisor to ensure that my asset allocation is correct, and then ride it out. ☐
e) Consider investing more because prices are so low. ☐

12. **Which of the following risks or events do you fear most?**
a) A loss of principal over any period of 1 year or less. ☐
b) A rate of inflation that exceeds my rate of return over the long term, because it will erode the purchasing power of my money. ☐
c) Portfolio performance that is insufficient to meet my goals. ☐
d) Portfolio performance that is consistently less than industry benchmarks. ☐
e) A missed investment opportunity that could have yielded higher returns over the long term, even though it entailed higher risk. ☐

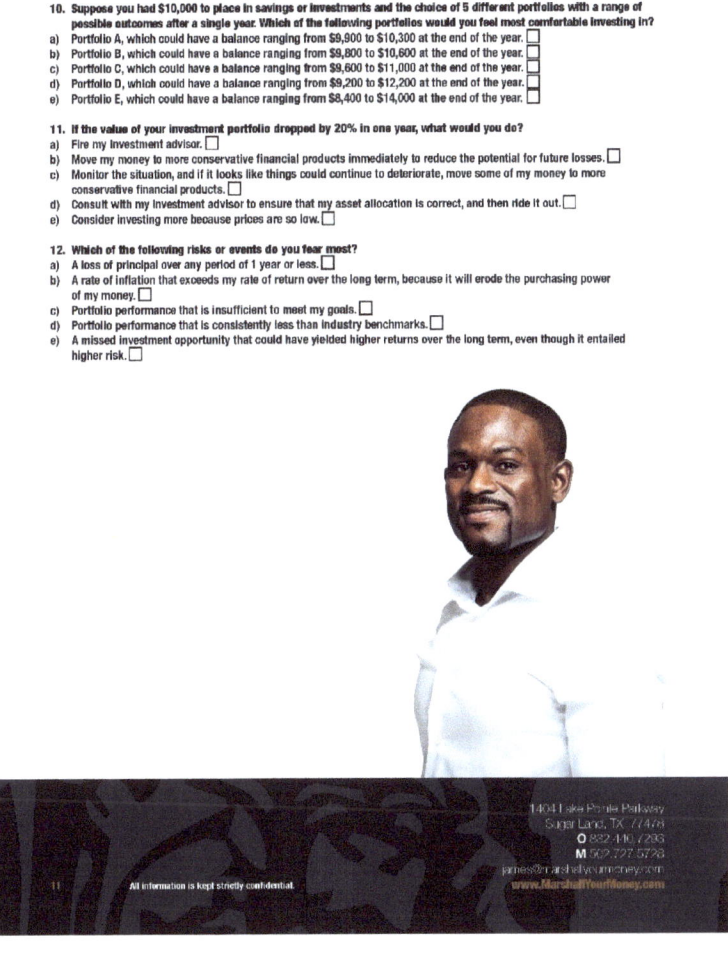

1404 Lake Pointe Parkway
Sugar Land, TX 77478
O 832-410-7293
M 502-727-5728
james@marshallyourmoney.com
www.MarshallYourMoney.com

11   All information is kept strictly confidential.

THE HIVE | 101

SCORING

Give the following points for each answer: $a = 1, b = 2, c = 3, d = 4, e = 5$

Question Number	My Answer	Point Value
Life Stage Questions		
1		
2		
Life Stage Score (add results from 1 and 2)		
Financial Resources and Emotional Risk Tolerance Questions		
3		
4		
5		
6		
7		
8		
9		
10		
11		
12		
Resources and Tolerance Score (add results from 3 thru 12)		

MARSHALL
Wealth Management, LLC
A Registered Investment Advisory Firm

All information is kept strictly confidential.

James L. Marshall, Jr. | 102

INTERPRETATION OF RESULTS

If your Life Stage Score is:	Then your Investment Time Horizon is:
1 to 3	Short-term (5 years or less)
4 to 6	Intermediate-term (5 to 10 years)
7 to 10	Long-term (over 10 years)

If your Investment Style Score is:	Then Your Investment Style is:
5 to 10	Very Conservative
11 to 20	Moderately Conservative
21 to 30	Moderate
31 to 40	Moderately Aggressive
41 to 50	Very Aggressive

1404 Lake Pointe Parkway
Sugar Land, TX 77478
O 832.440.7203
M 502.727.5726
james@marshallyourmoney.com
www.MarshallYourMoney.com

All information is kept strictly confidential.

THE HIVE | 103

BUILDING WEALTH ONE FAMILY AT A TIME!

- Individual & Family Comprehensive Financial Planning
- Investment Management
- Insurance (Life, Health, and Long-Term Care)
- Financial Education Services
- Institutional Money Management for Churches and 501c3s

- Retirement Planning
- Cash Management & Budgeting
- Family Trust, Charitable Giving, and Estate Planning

MARSHALL
Wealth Management, LLC
A Registered Investment Advisory Firm

Contact JAMES MARSHALL
For a complimentary consultation

1404 LAKE POINTE PKWY
SUGAR LAND, TX 77478
OFFICE: (832) 440-7293 | CELL: (502) 727-5728
JAMES@MARSHALLYOURMONEY.COM

WWW.MARSHALLYOURMONEY.COM

James L. Marshall, Jr. | 104